The Beaver Book of

CREEPY VERSE

Chosen by Ian and Zenka Woodward

Illustrated by William Geldart

First published in 1980 by
The Hamlyn Publishing Group Limited
London · New York · Sydney · Toronto
Astronaut House, Feltham, Middlesex, England
(Paperback Division: Hamlyn Paperbacks,
Banda House, Cambridge Grove,
Hammersmith, London W6 0LE)

© Copyright this collection
Ian and Zenka Woodward 1980
© Copyright illustrations
The Hamlyn Publishing Group Limited 1980
ISBN 0 600 20178 3

Set, printed and bound in England by
Cox and Wyman Limited, Reading
Set in Garamond

For our son
PHILIP
and his grandparents
NIAL and JEAN WOODWARD
and
FRANTIŠEK and HELENA LIŠKA
who have had their fair share of ghastly frights

Creepy?

'The night-wind rattles the window-frame. . . .'

So begins the very first creepy poem in a book
devoted to such creepy poems, and we are
immediately launched on a terrifying, spine-chilling
but wonderful, wonderful journey into the
supernatural world of the Unknown. We know all
about it. And so do you.

We all love to be scared! Some of us perhaps
wouldn't like to admit that we are frightened
by the idea of ghosts and vampires and werewolves
and things that make creepy noises at night when
we switch off the bedroom light. Oh no, of course
not! But most of us *are* troubled by such fears, no
matter how much we may try to put on a brave
face the next day and perhaps even joke about it.

Who has not felt an eerie, cold tingle run down
his spine when, all alone, he has gone into the garden
for something or other in the black depth of
evening? It is no joke *then*. The fiendish shadows
cast by a deathly white moon, the ominous rustle of
the bushes by the garden shed, the watchful 'eyes'
peering from behind (they are always *behind*). At such
times we are scared out of our wits by things that
cannot be seen as much as *felt*. It is all quite silly. Or is it?

There cannot be anyone reading this who has not woken up at night with a start, his heart pounding with the grim certainty that something *terrible* was present in the room, the response to which was probably to bury his head quickly under the bedcovers. How hot and suffocating that can be. And yet how comforting are those bedcovers as a much-needed protection against the darkened bedroom's most fearful shadows and creaky noises.

You will find plenty of poems in this collection about the scary things that can happen in the dead of night . . . and during the daytime, too. Spooks galore, stealing over the rooftop and across the ceiling and often making a nerve-racking 'bump' in the night, conspire to frighten us half to death.

But not only ghosts and poltergeists haunt these pages. As the church clock strikes midnight, we encounter witches flying on broomsticks on Hallowe'en night, and phantom dogs gnawing on bones in the graveyard, and saucer-eyed owls breaking the night's silence with their chilling '*Tu-whit-tu-whoos*'. You will be bewitched by devilish charms, spells, curses, riddles and gruesome epitaphs. Plus the odd – *very* odd – moontime monster.

We have gone in search of magic and mystery, and here is what we've found. A word of warning, though. *Be careful*. For who knows what, or who, may be lurking in the shadows just around the corner . . . ?

IAN AND ZENKA WOODWARD
Gallows Hill, King's Langley

All on my own

The night-wind rattles the window-frame –
I wake up shivering, shivering, all alone.
Darkness. Silence. What's the time?
Mother's asleep, and Dad's not home.
Shivering in the corner, shivering all alone.

Who's there – standing behind the curtain?
Shivering in the corner, no need to cry . . .
It's only the shadow of the tree in the garden
Shaking and sighing as the wind rushes by.
Shivering in the corner, and no need to cry.

Brian Lee

Who's that?

Who's that
stopping at
my door in the
dark, deep
in the dead of the moonless night?

Who's
that in the quiet
blackness,
darker than dark?

Who
turns the han-
dle of my door, who
turns the old brass hand-
le of
my door with never a sound, the handle
that always
creaks and rattles and
squeaks but
now
turns
without a sound, slowly
slowly
      slowly
            round?

Who's that moving through the floor
as if it were a lake, an open door? Who
is it who passes through
what can never be passed through,
who passes through
the rocking-chair
without rocking it,
who passes through
the table without knocking it, who
 walks out of the cupboard without unlocking it?
Who's that? Who plays with my toys
with no noise, no
noise?

Who's that? Who is it
silent and silver
as things in mirrors, who's
as slow as feathers,
shy as the shivers,
light as a fly?

Who's that who's that
as close as
close as a hug, a kiss –

Who's THIS?

James Kirkup

Seeing creepy things at night

I ain't afraid of snakes or rats or worms or mice,
And things what *girls* are skeered at I think are
                                                    awful nice.
I'm pretty brave I guess, and yet I hates to go to bed,
For when I'm tucked up warm and snug, and when
                                        my prayers are said,
Mother tells me happy dreams, and she takes away
                                            the light
And leaves me lying all alone a-seeing things at night.

Sometimes they're in the corner, sometimes they're
                                            by the door,
Sometimes they're all a-standing in the middle of the
                                            floor;
Sometimes they are sitting down, sometimes they're
                                        walking round
So softly and so creepy-like they never makes a
                                            sound;
And sometimes they're as black as ink, and other
                                    times they're white,
But the colour ain't no different when you see things
                                            at night.

Once when I licked a fellow, what just moved down
                                        our street,
My father sent me up to bed without a bit to eat;
I woke up in the night and saw things a-standin' in a
                                            row

And looking at me cross-eyed and a-pointing at me
so —
Oh, my, I was so scared that time, I never slept a mite,
It's almost always when I'm bad I see things at night.

Lucky thing I ain't a girl, or I'd be scared to death.
Seeing I'm a boy — I just duck my head and holds
my breath,
And oh, I am so sorry I've been a naughty boy
And I promise I'll be better and I'll say my prayers
again.
Granma tells me that's the only way to make it right
When a fellow has been wicked and sees things at
night.

So now when other naughty boys would tempt me
into sin,
I try to squash the tempter's voice which urges me
within;
And when there's pie for supper and cakes what's
big and nice
I wants 'em — but I don't pass my plate again — not
more than twice;
No, I'd rather let starvation wipe me slowly out of
sight
Than I should keep a-livin' on a-seeing things at
night.

Eugene Field

The silent voices

When the dumb hour, clothed in black,
Brings the dreams about my bed,
Call me not so often back,
Silent voices of the dead,
Toward the lowland ways behind me,
And the sunlight that is gone!
Call me rather, silent voices,
Forward to the starry track
Glimmering up the heights beyond me,
On, and always on!

Alfred, Lord Tennyson

Gruesome

I was sitting in the sitting room
toying with some toys
when from a door marked 'GRUESOME'
There came a GRUESOME noise.

Cautiously I opened it
and there to my surprise
a little GRUE lay sitting
with tears in its eyes

'Oh little GRUE please tell me
what is it ails thee so?'
'Well I'm so small,' he sobbed,
'GRUESSES don't want to know.'

'Exercises are the answer,
Each morning you must DO SOME.'
He thanked me, smiled,
and do you know what?
The very next day he. . . .

Roger McGough

Nasty night

Whose are the hands you hear
Pulling the roof apart?
What stamps its hoof
Between the bedroom ceiling and the slates?

Roy Fuller

Bump!

Things that go 'bump!' in the night,
Should not really give one a fright.
It's the hole in each ear
That lets in the fear,
That, and the absence of light!

Spike Milligan

The dark

I feared the darkness as a boy;
And if at night I had to go
Upstairs alone I'd make a show
Of carrying on with those below
A dialogue of shouts and 'whats?'
So they'd be sure to save poor Roy
Were he attacked by vampire bats.

Or thugs or ghosts. But far less crude
Than criminal or even ghost
Behind a curtain or a post
Was what I used to dread the most –
The always-unseen bugaboo
Of black-surrounded solitude.
I dread it still at sixty-two.

Roy Fuller

The haunted child

Oh, I am haunted at my play
And haunted in my bed,
But does the spirit haunt the house
Or does it haunt my head?

It mutters often in my ear . . .
I know when it's about,
But is it whispering to get in
Or weeping to get out?

The outside rooms, these painted walls
Where I am washed and fed
Are nothing but the shadows cast
By rooms inside my head.

And in the house behind my eyes
I watch the world go by
Strong as a king until I hear
That thin and needling cry.

All shadows, shades and wicked imps,
All creatures of the gloom,
And pucks and pixies may appear
Haunting my outside room.

But oh, but oh, my inside rooms!
Let no ghosts wander there,
And Silence be the only guest
Between my chin and hair.

Margaret Mahy

The silent spinney

What's that rustling behind me?
Only a cat.
Thank goodness for that,
For I'm afraid of the darkness,
And these tall trees
Are silent and black,
And if ever I get out of here, mate,
I can tell you I'm not coming back.

There's a dark shadow out in the roadway,
See if there's someone behind that tree,
For I'm afraid of the darkness
And it might jump out at me.

My sisters are scared stiff of spiders,
My mother is frightened of mice,
But I'm afraid of the darkness,
I'm not coming this way twice.

Seamus Redmond

Eeka, Neeka

Eeka, Neeka, Leeka, Lee –
Here's a lock without a key;
Bring a lantern, bring a candle,
Here's a door without a handle;
Shine, shine, you old thief Moon,
Here's a door without a room;
Not a whisper, moth or mouse,
Key – lock – door – room: where's the house?

Say nothing, creep away,
And live to knock another day!

Walter de la Mare

House fear

Always – I tell you this they learned –
Always at night when they returned
To the lonely house from far away
To lamps unlighted and fire gone grey,
They learned to rattle the lock and key
To give whatever might chance to be
Warning and time to be off in flight:
And preferring the out- to the in-door night,
They learned to leave the house-door wide
Until they had lit the lamp inside.

Robert Frost

The riddle

'What is it that goes round and round the house'
The riddle began. A wolf, we thought, or a ghost?
Our cold backs turned to the chink in the kitchen
                                        shutter,
The range made our small scared faces warm as toast.

But now the cook is dead and the cooking, no doubt,
                                        electric,
No room for draught or dream, for child or mouse,
Though we, in another place, still put ourselves the
                                        question:
What *is* it that goes round and round the house?

Louis MacNeice

The listeners

'Is there anybody there?' said the Traveller,
    Knocking on the moonlit door;
And his horse in the silence champed the grasses
    Of the forest's ferny floor:

And a bird flew up out of the turret,
  Above the Traveller's head:
And he smote upon the door again a second time;
  'Is there anybody there?' he said.
But no one descended to the Traveller;
  No head from the leaf-fringed sill
Leaned over and looked into his grey eyes,
  Where he stood perplexed and still.
But only a host of phantom listeners
  That dwelt in the lone house then
Stood listening in the quiet of the moonlight
  To that voice from the world of men:
Stood thronging the faint moonbeams on the dark
                                        stair,
  That goes down to the empty hall,
Hearkening in an air stirred and shaken
  By the lonely Traveller's call.
And he felt in his heart, their strangeness,
  Their stillness answering his cry,
While his horse moved, cropping the dark turf,
  'Neath the starred and leafy sky;
For he suddenly smote on the door, even
  Louder, and lifted his head:
'Tell them I came, and no one answered,
  'That I kept my word,' he said.
Never the least stir made the listeners,
  Though every word he spake
Fell echoing through the shadowiness of the still house
  From the one man left awake:
Ay, they heard his foot upon the stirrup,
  And the sound of iron on stone,
And how the silence surged softly backward,
  When the plunging hoofs were gone.

Walter de la Mare

Daniel Webster's horses

If when the wind blows
Rattling the trees
Clicking like skeletons'
Elbows and knees,

You hear along the road
Three horses pass –
Do not go near the dark
Cold window glass.

If when the first snow lies
Whiter than bones
You see the mark of hoofs
Cut to the stones,

Hoofs of three horses
Going abreast –
Turn about, turn about,
A closed door is best!

Upright in the earth
Under the sod
They buried three horses
Bridled and shod,

Daniel Webster's horses –
He said as he grew old,
'Flesh, I loved riding,
Shall I not love it, cold?

'Shall I not love to ride
Bone astride bone,
When the cold wind blows
And snow covers stone?

'Bury them on their feet
With bridle and bit.
They were fine horses –
See their shoes fit.'

Elizabeth Coatsworth

The queer moment

It was a queer moment when all on my own
   I woke up in the gloom
To hear, far away, the bell of a church
   Go *boom, boom, boom*.

It was a queer minute when something in the walls
   Scampered and scampered, on and on,
And the wind whimpered about the house
   Please, please let me in . . . .

It was a queer hour as I listened to the clock
   Tick-tock, fidget on the wall,
And my breath wouldn't come, and my heart knock-
                   knocked
   For no reason at all.

Brian Lee

Quite in the dark

I woke up to the blackness,
The silence of perfect night –
As black as it was silent,
  No sound, no sign of light:

I dared not cross the carpet,
To find the light-switch on the wall –
I lay dead still, as though tied down –
  And couldn't move at all;

As though the dark pressed on my legs,
As though the blanket weighed like lead,
As though the silence kept my arms
  Pinned on to my bed.

But, though they were the oddest moments,
My thoughts were odder by far,
And the words that kept coming to me
    Were oddly circular.

They were: 'I wonder who I am?'
And next: 'And where did I come from?'
And then: 'Why am I me and not
    Dick, or Harry, or Tom?'

Then I demanded, loud and clear,
Though trembling at my daring –
'Who or what was it, made me, *me*,
    And not some other thing?'

But the dark answered with no sound,
And gave me nothing to see,
As smothering as too many blankets,
    And just as still as me.

And the more I thought and thought, the more
The words went around and around,
The more and more I *had* to know
    The answer I never found –

For as my brains went round and round,
They went down, deep, deep, deep.
And before I could *quite* work it out,
    I dropped back to sleep.

                                    Brian Lee

In the night

There always is a noise when it is dark!
It is the noise of silence, and the noise
Of blindness!

The noise of silence, and the noise of blindness
Do frighten me!
They hold me stark and rigid as a tree!

These frighten me!
These hold me stark and rigid as a tree!
Because at last their tumult is more loud
Than thunder!

Because
Their tumult is more loud than thunder
They terrify my soul! They tear
My heart asunder!

James Stephens

Night omens

Impinging on the cocoon of sleep:
The heavy breathing of the sea;
The interminable chirping of crickets;
The drunken return of revellers;
A great dog gnawing on bones
In a deserted side street.

John Cotton

Bad dream

The window was made of ice with bears lumbering
                                        across it,
        Bears the size of flies;
The ceiling was one great web with flies cantankering
                                        in it,
        Flies the size of men;
The floor was riddled with holes with men
                        phutscuttering down them
        Into the jaws of mice.

Outside there were no other houses, only bedizened
                                        hoardings
        With panties prancing on them
And an endless file of chromium-plated lamp posts
        With corpses dangling from them
And one gaunt ruined church with a burglar alarm
                                        filibustering
        High and dry in the steeple.

Here then the young man came who wanted to eat
                                        and drink,
        To play, pray, make love;
Electronic voices nagged at him out of the filtered air,
        The eyes on the hoarding winked;
He knocked at the door of the house, the bears
                                buzzed and the flies
        Howled to him to come in.

Inside he found a table laid for two, a mirror
    Flanking the double bed,
On the night table a scent spray, a tin of biscuits, a
                            bible,
    A crucifix on the wall
And beside it a comic postcard: all this he carefully
                          noticed
    And then he noticed the floor

Bomb-pocked with tiny holes, from one of which
                       there rose
    One tiny wisp of white.
He watched as it clawed the air two inches from the
                         floor
    And saw it for what it was,
The arm of a girl, he watched and just could hear
                      her voice
    Say: Wait! Wait till I grow.

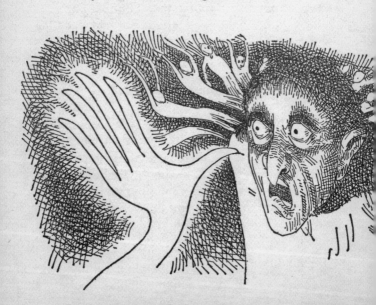

And the arm grew and he wished to bend and clutch
>> the hand
>> But found he could no more move,
The arm grew and the fingers groped for help, the
>> voice
>> That had grown with the arm, the voice
That was now a woman's about to be saved or lost
>> was calling
>> For help. He could not move.

Then everything buzzed and boomed. The chaps
>> outside on the lamp posts
>> Hooted, broke wind, and wept,
Men the size of flies dropped down his neck while
>> the mansized
>> Flies gave just three cheers
And he could not move. The darkness under the
>> floor gave just
>> One shriek. The arm was gone.

Louis MacNeice

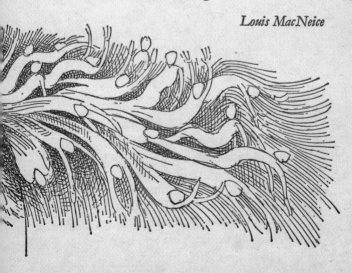

Moths and moonshine

Moths and moonshine mean to me
Magic — madness — mystery.

Witches dancing weird and wild
Mischief make for man and child.

Owls screech from woodland shades,
Moths glide through moonlit glades,

Moving in dark and secret wise
Like a plotter in disguise.

Moths and moonshine mean to me
Magic — madness — mystery.

James Reeves

The witch's song

'Hoity-Toity! Hop-o'-my-Thumb!
Tweedledee and Tweedledum!
All hobgoblins come to me,
Over the mountains, over the sea;
Come in a hurry, come in a crowd,
Flying, chattering, shrieking loud;
I and my broomstick fidget and call –
Come, hobgoblins, we want you all!

'I have a pot of a mischievous brew;
You must do what I tell you to:
Blow through the keyholes, hang to the eaves,
Litter the garden with dead brown leaves;
Into the houses hustle and run,
Here is mischief and here is fun!
Break the china and slam the doors,
Crack the windows and scratch the floors,
Let in the cockroaches, mice and rats,
Sit on the family's Sunday hats;
Hiding and stealing everything little,
Smashing everything thin and brittle:
Teasing the children, tickling their heels –
Look at them jumping! Hark to their squeals!
Pinch their elbows and pull their hair,
Then out again to the gusty air!

'Flutter the birds in their sheltered nests,
Pluck the down from the ducklings' breasts,
Steal the eggs from the clucking hen.

'Ride the pigs round and round the pen!
Here is mischief to spare for all –
Hoity-toity, come at my call!
Tweedledum and Tweedledee,
Come at my summons – come to me!'

Thus said a witch on a windy night,
Then sailed on her broomstick out of sight.

Ruth Bedford

I saw three witches

I saw three witches
That bowed down like barley,
And took to their brooms 'neath a louring sky,
And, mounting a storm-cloud,
Aloft on its margin,
Stood black in the silver as up they did fly.

I saw three witches
That mocked the poor sparrows
They carried in cages of wicker along,
Till a hawk from his eyrie
Swooped down like an arrow,
And smote on the cages, and ended their song.

I saw three witches
That sailed in a shallop
All turning their heads with a truculent smile
Till a bank of green osiers
Concealed their grim faces,
Though I heard them lamenting for many a mile.

I saw three witches
Asleep in a valley,
Their heads in a row, like stones in a flood,
Till the moon, creeping upward,
Looked white through the valley,
And turned them to bushes in bright scarlet bud.

Walter de la Mare

Night clouds

The white mares of the moon rush along the sky
Beating their golden hoofs upon the glass Heavens;
The white mares of the moon are all standing on
                                    their hind legs
Pawing at the green porcelain doors of the remote
                                    Heavens.

Fly, mares!
Strain your utmost,
Scatter the milky dust of stars,
Or the tiger sun will leap upon you and destroy you
With one lick of his vermilion tongue.

Amy Lowell

Old Moll

The moon is up,
  The night owls scritch.
Who's that croaking?
  The frog in the ditch.
Who's that howling?
  The old hound bitch.
My neck tingles,
  My elbows itch,
My hair rises,
  My eyelids twitch.
What's in that pot
  So rare and rich?
Who's that crouching
  In a cloak like pitch?
Hush! that's Old Moll –
  They say she's a
Most ree-markable old party.

James Reeves

Owl

On Midsummer night the witches shriek,
The frightened fairies swoon,
The nightjar mutters in his sleep
And ghosts around the chimney creep.
The loud winds cry, the fir trees crash,
And the owl stares at the moon.

Sylvia Read

Riddle

What a hideous crackling and whistling
Interrupt my sleep!
I open the curtains. What do I see and hear? ...
Two brooms brushing the tree-tops,
Two cloaks blowing in the wind,
Two cats holding tight,
Two jockeys shouting,
'I'll beat you to the moon! I'll beat you to the moon!'

I wonder *which* will win.

Ian Serraillier

Answer: two witches

Space traveller

There was a witch, hump-backed and hooded,
  Lived by herself in a burnt-out tree.
When storm winds shrieked and the moon was buried
  And the dark of the forest was black as black,
  She rose in the air like a rocket at sea,
      Riding the wind,
      Riding the night,
  Riding the tempest to the moon and back.

James Nimmo

The ride-by-nights

Up on their brooms the Witches stream,
Crooked and black in the crescent's gleam;
One foot high, and one foot low,
Bearded, cloaked, and cowled, they go.

'Neath Charlie's Wain they twitter and tweet,
And away they swarm 'neath the Dragon's feet,
With a whoop and a flutter they swing and sway,
And surge pell-mell down the Milky Way.

Between the legs of the glittering Chair
They hover and squeak in the empty air.
Then round they swoop past the glimmering Lion
To where Sirius barks behind huge Orion;
Up, then, and over to wheel amain
Under the silver, and home again.

Walter de la Mare

When shall we three meet again?

(*from* Macbeth)

First Witch: When shall we three meet again
In thunder, lightning, or in rain?
Second Witch: When the hurlyburly's done,
When the battle's lost and won.
Third Witch: That will be ere the set of sun.
First Witch: Where the place?
Second Witch: Upon the heath.
Third Witch: There to meet with Macbeth.
First Witch: I come, Graymalkin!
Second Witch: Paddock calls.
Third Witch: Anon.
All: Fair is foul, and foul is fair:
Hover through the fog and filthy air.

William Shakespeare

The witch's cat

'My magic is dead,' said the witch. 'I'm astounded
That people can fly to the moon and around it.
It used to be mine and the cat's till they found it.
My broomstick is draughty, I snivel with cold
As I ride to the stars. I'm painfully old,
   And so is my cat;
   But planet-and-space-ship,
   Rocket or race-ship
Never shall part me from that.'

She wrote an advertisement, 'Witch in a fix
Willing to part with the whole bag of tricks,
Going cheap at the price at eighteen and six.'
But no one was ready to empty his coffers
For out-of-date rubbish. There weren't any offers –
   Except for the cat.
   'But planet-and-space-ship,
   Rocket or race-ship
Never shall part me from that.'

The tears trickled fast, not a sentence she spoke
As she stamped on her broom and the brittle stick
                              broke,
And she dumped in a dustbin her hat and her cloak,
Then clean disappeared, leaving no prints;
And no one at all has set eyes on her since
   Or her tired old cat.
   'But planet-and-space-ship,
   Rocket or race-ship
Never shall part me from that.'

Ian Serraillier

Thrice the brinded cat hath mew'd

(*from* Macbeth)

First Witch: Thrice the brinded cat hath mew'd.
Second Witch: Thrice, and once the hedge-pig whined.
Third Witch: Harpier cries: 'Tis time, 'tis time.
First Witch: Round about the cauldron go;
   In the poisoned entrails throw.
   Toad, that under cold stone

Days and nights hast thirty-one
Sweltered venom sleeping got,
Boil thou first in the charmed pot.

All: Double, double toil and trouble;
Fire, burn; and, cauldron, bubble.

Second Witch: Fillet of a fenny snake,
In the cauldron boil and bake;
Eye of newt, and toe of frog,
Wool of bat, and tongue of dog,
Adder's fork, and blind-worms' sting,
Lizard's leg, and howlet's wing,
For a charm of powerful trouble;
Like a hell-broth boil and bubble.

All: Double, double toil and trouble,
Fire, burn; and, cauldron, bubble.

Third Witch: Scale of dragon, tooth of wolf,
Witches' mummy, maw and gulf
Of the ravined salt-sea shark,
Root of hemlock digged in the dark,
Liver of blaspheming Jew,
Gall of goat, and slips of yew
Slivered in the moon's eclipse,
Nose of Turk, and Tartar's lips,
Finger of birth-strangled babe
Ditch-delivered by a drab,
Make the gruel thick and slab:
Add thereto a tiger's chaudron,
For the ingredients of our cauldron.

All: Double, double toil and trouble;
Fire, burn; and, cauldron, bubble.

Second Witch: Cool it with a baboon's blood,
Then the charm is firm and good.

William Shakespeare

The little creature

Twinkum, twankum, twirlum and twitch –
My great grandam – She was a Witch;
Mouse in wainscot, Saint in niche –
My great grandam – She was a Witch;
Deadly nightshade flowers in a ditch –
My great grandam – She was a Witch;
Long though the shroud, it grows stitch by stitch –
My great grandam – She was a Witch;
Wean you weakling before you breech –
My great grandam – She was a Witch;
The fattest pig's but a double flitch –
My great grandam – She was a Witch;
Nightjars rattle, owls scritch –
My great grandam – She was a Witch.

    Pretty and small,
    A mere nothing at all,
    Pinned up sharp in the ghost of a shawl,
    She'd straddle her down to the kirkyard wall,
    And mutter and whisper and call,
    And call. . . .

Red blood out and black blood in,
My Nannie says I'm a child of sin.
How did I choose me my witchcraft kin?
Know I as soon as dark's dreams begin
Snared is my heart in a nightmare's gin;
Never from terror I out may win;
So dawn and dusk I pine, peak, thin,
Scarcely knowing t'other from which –
My great grandam – She was a Witch.

Walter de la Mare

The witch stepmother

'I was but seven year old
   When my mother she did die;
My father married the very worst woman
   The world did ever see.

For she has made me the loathly worm
   That lies at the foot of the tree,
And my sister Maisry she's made
   The mackerel of the sea.

And every Saturday at noon
   The mackerel comes to me,
And she takes my loathly head
   And lays it on her knee,
She combs it with a silver comb,
   And washes it in the sea.

Seven knights have I slain,
   Since I lay at the foot of the tree,
And were you not my own father,
   The eighth one you should be.'

The father sent for his lady,
   As fast as send could he:
'Where is my son that you sent from me,
   And my daughter Lady Maisry?'

'Your son is at our king's court,
   Serving for meat and fee;
And your daughter's at our queen's court,
   A waiting-woman is she.'

'You lie, you ill woman,
  So loud I hear you lie:
My son's the loathly worm,
  That lies at the foot of the tree,
And my daughter Lady Maisry
  Is the mackerel of the sea!'

She has taken a silver wand,
  And given him strokes three,
And he's started up the bravest knight
  That ever your eyes did see.

She has taken a small horn,
  And loud and shrill blew she,
And all the fish came unto her
  But the proud mackerel of the sea:
'You shaped me once an unseemly shape
  You shall never more shape me.'

He has sent to the wood
  For whins and for hawthorn,
And he has taken that gay lady
And there he did her burn.

Unknown

Kitchen song

Grey as a guinea-fowl is the rain
Squawking down from the boughs again.
     'Anne, Anne,
      Go fill the pail,'
Said the old witch who sat on the rail.
'Though there is a hole in the bucket,
Anne, Anne,
It will fill my pocket;
The water-drops when they cross my doors
Will turn to guineas and gold moidores. . . .'
The well-water hops across the floors;
Whimpering, 'Anne' it cries, implores,
And the guinea-fowl-plumaged rain,
Squawking down from the boughs again,
Cried, 'Anne, Anne, go fill the bucket,
There is a hole in the witch's pocket –
And the water-drops like gold moidores,
Obedient girl, will surely be yours.
So, Anne, Anne,
Go fill the pail
Of the old witch who sits on the rail!'

Edith Sitwell

Two witches

There was a witch
The witch had an itch
The itch was so itchy it
Gave her a twitch.

Another witch
Admired the twitch
So she started twitching
Though she had no itch.

Now both of them twitch
So it's hard to tell which
Witch has the itch and
Which witch has the twitch.

Alexander Resnikoff

Hinx, minx, the old witch winks

Hinx, minx, the old witch winks,
The fat begins to fry.
Nobody at home but jumping Joan,
Father, mother and I.
Stick, stock, stone dead,
Blind man can't see;
Every knave will have a slave,
You and I must be he.

Unknown

The witch's house

Its wicked little windows leer
   Beneath a mouldy thatch,
And village children come and peer
   Before they lift the latch.

A one-eyed crow hops to the door,
   Fat spiders crowd the pane,
And dark herbs scattered on the floor
   Waft fragrance down the lane.

It sits so low, the little hutch,
   So secret, shy and squat,
As if in its mysterious clutch
   It nursed one knew not what

That beggars passing by the ditch
   Are haunted with desire
To force the door, and see the witch
   Vanish in flames of fire.

Laura Benét

The witch

I have walked a great while over the snow,
And I am not tall nor strong.
My clothes are wet, and my teeth are set,
And the way was hard and long.
I have wandered over the fruitful earth,
But I never came here before.
Oh, lift me over the threshold, and let me in at the
door!

The cutting wind is a cruel foe.
I dare not stand in the blast.
My hands are stone, and my voice a groan,
And the worst of death is past.
I am but a little maiden still,
My little white feet are sore.
Oh, lift me over the threshold, and let me in at the
door!

Her voice was the voice that women have,
Who plead for their heart's desire.
She came – she came – and the quivering flame
Sank and died in the fire.
It never was lit again on my hearth
Since I hurried across the floor,
To lift her over the threshold, and let her in at the
door.

Mary Coleridge

The witch

You, browed maiden, your eyes' bright pictures have
                                              caught me
    And I have changed into another man
—She bound her brows in a scarlet kerchief, she
                                              bound
        Her breasts in a velvet bodice's span
She slowly closed her eyes upon me, and I
Having no time to bridle my horse, ran
        Whither I know not – where am I?

D. H. Lawrence

The two witches

O, sixteen hundred and ninety one,
Never was year so well begun,
Backsy-forsy and inside-out,
The best of all years to ballad about.

On the first fine day of January
I ran to my sweetheart Margery
And tossed her over the roof so far
That down she fell like a shooting star.

But when we two had frolicked and kissed
She clapped her fingers about my wrist
And tossed me over the chimney stack,
And danced on me till my bones did crack.

Then, when she had laboured to ease my pain,
We sat by the stile of Robin's Lane,
She in a hare and I in a toad
And puffed at the clouds till merry they glowed.

We spelled our loves until close of day.
I wished her good-night and walked away,
But she put out a tongue that was long and red
And swallowed me down like a crumb of bread.

Robert Graves

45

Alison Gross

O Alison Gross that lives in yon tower,
  The ugliest witch in the north country,
Has trysted me one day up to her bower,
  And many fair speeches she made to me.

She stroked my head and she combed my hair,
  And she set me down softly on her knee;
Says, 'If you will be my sweetheart so true,
  So many fine things I will give to thee.'

She showed me a mantle of red scarlet,
  With golden flowers and fringes fine;
Says, 'If you will be my sweetheart so true,
  This goodly gift it shall be thine.'

'Away, away, you ugly witch,
  Hold far away, and let me be!
I never will be your sweetheart so true,
  And I wish I were out of your company.'

She next brought a shirt of the softest silk,
  Well wrought with pearls about the band;
Says, 'If you will be my sweetheart so true,
  This goodly gift you shall command.'

She showed me a cup of the good red gold,
  Well set with jewels so fair to see;
Says, 'If you will be my sweetheart so true,
  This goodly gift I will give to thee.'

'Away, away, you ugly witch,
  Hold far away, and let me be!

I would not once kiss your ugly mouth
   For all the gold in the north country.'

She's turned her right and round about,
   And thrice she blew on a grass-green horn;
And she swore by the moon and the stars above
   That she'd make me rue the day I was born.

Then out she has taken a silver wand,
   And she's turned her three times round and round;
She muttered such words that my strength it failed
   And I fell down senseless on the ground.

She's turned me into an ugly worm,
   And made me toddle about the tree;
And aye, on every Saturday night,
   My sister Maisry came to me,

With silver basin and silver comb,
   To comb my headie upon her knee;
But before I'd have kissed with Alison Gross,
   I'd sooner have toddled about the tree.

But as it fell out, on last Hallowe'en,
   When the Fairy Court came riding by,
The Queen lighted down on a flowery bank,
   Not far from the tree where I used to lie.

She took me up in her milk-white hand,
   And she's stroked me three times over her knee;
She changed me again to my own proper shape,
   And no more I toddle about the tree.

Old English ballad

Hallowe'en

This is the night when witches fly
On their whizzing broomsticks through the wintry
sky;
Steering up the pathway where the stars are strewn,
They stretch skinny fingers to the waking moon.

This is the night when old wives tell
Strange and creepy stories, tales of charm and spell;
Peering at the pictures flaming in the fire
They wait for whispers from a ghostly choir.

This is the night when angels go
In and out of the houses winging o'er the snow;
Clearing out the demons from the countryside
They make it new and ready for Christmastide.

Leonard Clark

Hay-how for Hallowe'en!

Hay-how for Hallowe'en!
And the witches to be seen,
Some black, and some green,
Hey-how for Hallowe'en!

Unknown

Hallowe'en

Ruth says Apples have learned to bob.
Bob says Pumpkins have a job.
　　　Here's the man from the Witching Tree.
　　　Ask *him* since you won't ask me:
Do you think Ruth is telling the truth?

'Man from the Tree, your skin is green,
What night is this?' 'It's Hallowe'en.'

Ruth, Ruth, you told the truth.
The man says Apples *have* learned to bob.
The man says Pumpkins *do* have a job.
The man come down from the Witching Tree
Says he wants someone. No, not me.
Says he wants someone good and true –
　　　YOU!

Mother, Mother, Ruth's gone flying!
Hush, children, stop that crying.

Mother, mother, she's up in The Tree!
Climb up and tell me what you see.

Mother, she's higher than I can climb!
She'll be back by breakfast time.

Mother, what if she's gone for good?
She'll have to make do with witches' food.

Mother, what do witches eat?
Milk and potatoes and YOU, my sweet.

　　　　　　　　　　　　　　　　John Ciardi

The turn of the road

I was playing with my hoop along the road
Just where the bushes are, when, suddenly,
I heard a shout.—I ran away and stowed
Myself beneath a bush, and watched to see
What made the noise, and then, around the bend,
A woman came.

She was old.
She was wrinkle-faced. She had big teeth.—The end
Of her red shawl caught on a bush and rolled
Right off her and her hair fell down.—Her face
Was white, and awful, and her eyes looked sick,
And she was talking queer.

'*O God of Grace!*'
Said she, '*Where is the child?*' And flew back quick
The way she came, and screamed, and shook her
hands!
. . . Maybe she was a witch from foreign lands.

James Stephens

All, all a-lonely

Three little children sitting on the sand,
All, all a-lonely,
Three little children sitting on the sand,
All, all a-lonely,
Down in the green wood shady –
There came an old woman, said, 'Come on with me,'
All, all a-lonely,
There came an old woman, said, 'Come on with me,'
All, all a-lonely,
Down in the green wood shady –
She stuck her pen-knife through their heart,
All, all a-lonely,
She stuck her pen-knife through their heart,
All, all a-lonely,
Down in the green wood shady.

Unknown

Look out, boys!

Look out! Look out, boys! Clear the track!
The witches are here! They've all come back!
They hanged them high – No use! No use!
What cares a witch for the hangman's noose?
They buried them deep, but they wouldn't lie still,
For cats and witches are hard to kill;
They swore they shouldn't and wouldn't die –
Books said they did, but they lie! they lie!

Oliver Wendell Holmes

Three witches' charms

Charm 1
Dame, dame! the watch is set:
Quickly come, we all are met.
From the lakes and from the fens,
From the rocks and from the dens,
From the woods and from the caves,
From the churchyards, from the graves,
From the dungeon, from the tree
That they die on, here are we!

        Comes she not yet?
        Strike another heat!

Charm 2
The weather is fair, the wind is good:
Up, dame, on your horse of wood!
Or else tuck up your grey frock,
And saddle your goat or your green cock,
And make his bridle a bottom of thrid
To roll up how many miles you have rid.
Quickly come away,
For we all stay.

        Not yet? no then
        We'll try her again.

Charm 3

The owl is abroad, the bat and the toad,
  And so is the cat-a-mountain;
The ant and the mole sit both in a hole,
  And frog peeps out of the fountain.
The dogs they do bay, and the timbrels play,
  The spindle is now a-turning;
The moon it is red, and the stars are fled,
  But all the sky is a-burning:
The ditch is made, and our nails the spade:
With pictures full, of wax and of wool,
Their livers I stick with needles quick;
There lacks but the blood to make up the flood.
Quickly, dame, then bring your part in!
Spur, spur, upon little Martin!
Merrily, merrily, make him sail,
A worm in his mouth and a thorn in's tail,
Fire above, and fire below,
With a whip in your hand to make him go!

      O now she's come!
      Let all be dumb.

Ben Jonson

Witch's milking charm

    Meares' milk, and deer's milk,
    And every beast that bears milk
    Between St Johnston and Dundee,
    Come a' to me, come a' to me.

Unknown

Charm

Bring the holy crust of bread,
Lay it underneath the head;
It's a certain charm to keep
Hags away, while children sleep.

Robert Herrick

A witch's chant

The tail of a rat,
The hair of a cat,
The tooth from a jaw,
A rabbit's fore-paw,
The head of a gnat,
The wings of a bat,
All stirred to make magic
And things that are tragic.

John Wilson

Witch's broomstick spell

Horse and hattock,
Horse and go,
Horse and pelatis, Ho, ho!

Unknown

Spells

(to be said to a balloon being blown up)

Love me, you'll grow fat and fly,
Hate me, you'll grow thin and die.
Sail, O sail the windy sky!
    Hate me, thinner,
    Nothing for dinner;
    Love me, fatter,
    Butter and batter.
Fatter, fatter, fatter, fatter –

    B A N G !

Ian Serraillier

A spell to destroy life

Listen!
   Now I have come to step over your soul
      (I know your clan)
      (I know your name)
      (I have stolen your spit and buried it under earth)
   I bury your soul under earth
   I cover you over with black rock
   I cover you over with black cloth
   I cover you over with black slabs
   You disappear forever

   Your path leads to the
      Black Coffin
      in the hills of the Darkening Land

So let it be for you

   The clay of the hills covers you
   The black clay of the Darkening Land

   Your soul fades away

   It becomes blue (colour of despair)
   When darkness comes your spirit shrivels and
      dwindles to disappear forever
Listen!

Cherokee Indians,
North America

Kehama's curse

I charm thy life
From the weapons of strife,
From stone and from wood,
From fire and from flood,
From the serpent's tooth,
And the beasts of blood:
From sickness I charm thee,
And time shall not harm thee;
But earth which is mine,
Its fruits shall deny thee;
And water shall hear me,
And know thee and fly thee;
And the winds shall not touch thee
When they pass by thee,
And the dews shall not wet thee,
When they fall nigh thee:
And thou shalt seek death
To release thee, in vain;
Thou shalt live in thy pain
While Kehama shall reign,
With a fire in thy heart,
And a fire in thy brain;
And sleep shall obey me,
And visit thee never,
And the curse shall be on thee
For ever and ever.

Robert Southey

The witch's work song

Two spoons of sherry
Three ounces of yeast,
Half a pound of unicorn,
And God bless the feast.
Shake them in the collander,
Bang them to a chop,
Simmer slightly, snip up nicely,
Jump, skip, hop.
Knit one, knot one, purl two together,
Pip one and pop one and pluck the secret feather.

Baste in a mod. oven.
God bless our coven.
Tra-la-la!
Three toads in a jar.
Te-he-he!
Put in the frog's knee.
Peep out of the lace curtain.
There goes the Toplady girl, she's up to no good
that's certain.

Oh, what a lovely baby!
How nice it would go with gravy.
Pinch the salt,
Turn the malt
With a hey-nonny-nonny and I don't mean maybe.

T. H. White

'... The curse be ended'

'Round and round the circle
Completing the charm
So the knot be unknotted
The cross be uncrossed
The crooked be made straight
And the curse be ended.'

T. S. Eliot

Against witches

Black luggie, lammer bead,
Rowan-tree, and red thread,
Put the witches to their speed.

Unknown

The witches' song

'I have been all day looking after
A raven feeding upon a quarter;
And, soon as she turned her back to the south,
I snatched this morsel out of her mouth.'

'I last night lay all alone
On the ground, to hear the mandrake groan;
And plucked him up, though he grew full low:
And, as I had done, the cock did crow.'

'And I had been plucking (plants among)
Hemlock, henbane, adder's-tongue,
Nightshade, moonwort, libbard's-bane;
And twice by the dogs was like to be ta'en.'

'Yes, I have brought, to help your vows,
Horned poppy, cypress boughs.
The fig-tree wild, that grows on tombs,
And juice that from the larch-tree comes,
The basilisk's blood, and the viper's skin;
And now our orgies let's begin.'

Ben Jonson

The two ravens

As I was walking all alone,
I heard two ravens cry and moan:
I heard the one to the other say,
'Where shall we go and dine today?'

'In the ditch below the field
There lies a knight that's newly killed;
And nobody knows that he lies there
But his hawk, his hound, and his lady fair.

'His hound has gone to hunt the deer,
His hawk has flown to the empty air,
His lady's found another man;
So we'll have dinner while we can.

'His white neck-bone will be your prize,
And I'll pick out his two blue eyes;
With one lock of his golden hair
We'll line our nest, when it is bare.

'Many a man for him will mourn,
But none shall know where he has gone;
Over his bones, when they are bare,
The wind shall blow for evermore.'

Ian Serraillier

A croon on Hennacliff

Thus said the rushing raven,
  Unto his hungry mate:
'Ho! gossip! for Bude Haven:
  There be corpses six or eight.
Cawk! Cawk! the crew and skipper
  Are wallowing in the sea:
So there's a savoury supper
  For my old dame and me.'

'Cawk! gaffer! thou art dreaming,
  The shore hath wreckers bold;
Would rend the yelling seamen,
  From the clutching billows' hold.
Cawk! Cawk! they'd bound for booty
  Into the dragon's den:
And shout, for "death or duty",
  If the prey were drowning men.'

Loud laughed the listening surges,
  At the guess our grandame gave:
You might call them Boanerges,
  From the thunder of their wave.
And mockery followed after
  The sea-bird's jeering brood:
That filled the skies with laughter,
  From Lundy Light to Bude.

'Cawk! cawk!' then said the raven,
  'I am fourscore years and ten:
Yet never in Bude Haven,
  Did I croak for rescued men.
They will save the Captain's girdle,
  And shirt, if shirt there be:
But leave their blood to curdle,
  For my old dame and me.'

So said the rushing raven,
  Unto his hungry mate:
'Ho! gossip! for Bude Haven:
  There be corpses six or eight.
Cawk! cawk! the crew and skipper
  Are wallowing in the sea:
O what a savoury supper
  For my old dame and me.'

                    Robert Stephen Hawker

White witchcraft

If you and I could change to beasts, what beast
                                should either be?
Shall you and I play Jove for once? Turn fox then,
                                I decree!
Shy wild sweet stealer of the grapes! Now do your
                                worst on me!

And thus you think to spite your friend – turned
                                loathsome? What, a toad?
So, all men shrink and shun me! Dear men, pursue
                                your road!
Leave but my crevice in the stone, a reptile's fit
                                abode!

                                        Robert Browning

Charm against an egg-boat

*According to an old superstition, when a boiled egg had
been eaten, the spoon at once had to be put through the end
of the shell that was not yet broken. This was believed to
prevent witches from going to sea in unbroken shells and
brewing up storms.)*

You must break the shell to bits, for fear
The witches should make it a boat, my dear:
For over the sea, away from home,
Far by night the witches roam.

                                        Unknown

The Egg-shell

The wind took off with the sunset –
The fog came up with the tide,
When the Witch of the North took an Egg-shell
With a little Blue Devil inside.
'Sink,' she said, 'or swim,' she said,
'It's all you will get from me.
And that is the finish of *him*!' she said,
And the Egg-shell went to sea.

The wind fell dead with the midnight –
The fog shut down like a sheet,
When the Witch of the North heard the Egg-shell
Feeling by hand for a fleet.
'Get!' she said, 'or you're gone,' she said,
But the little Blue Devil said 'No!'
'The sights are just coming on,' he said,
And he let the Whitehead go.

The wind got up with the morning –
The fog blew off with the rain,
When the Witch of the North saw the Egg-shell
And the little Blue Devil again.
'Did you swim?' she said. 'Did you sink?' she said,
And the little Blue Devil replied:
'For myself I swam, but I *think*,' he said,
'There's somebody sinking outside.'

Rudyard Kipling

The hag

The hag is astride,
  This night for to ride;
The Devil and she together:
  Through thick and through thin,
  Now out and then in,
Though ne'er so foul be the weather.

A thorn or a burr
  She takes for a spur:
With a lash of a bramble she rides now,
  Through brakes and through briars,
  O'er ditches and mires,
She follows the spirit that guides now.

No beast, for his food,
  Dares now range the wood;
But hushed in his lair he lies lurking:
  While mischiefs, by these,
  On land and on seas,
At noon of night are a-working.

The storm will arise
  And trouble the skies;
This night, and more for the wonder,
  The ghost from the tomb
  Affrighted shall come,
Called out by the clap of the thunder.

Robert Herrick

A curse

Bruadar and Smith and Glinn
   Amen, dear God, I pray,
May they lie low in waves of woe,
   And tortures slow each day!
             Amen! ...

Bruadar and Smith and Glinn
   May flails of sorrow flay!
Cause for lamenting, snares and cares
   Be theirs for night and day!
             Amen! ...

For Bruadar gape the grave,
   Up-shovel for Smith the mould,
Amen, O King of the Sunday! Leave
   Glinn in the Devil's hold.
             Amen!

Douglas Hyde

On a Lord

Here lies the Devil – ask no other name.
Well – but you mean Lord——? Hush! we mean the
                     same.

Samuel Taylor Coleridge

The Devil

From his brimstone bed at break of day
A-walking the Devil is gone,
To visit his snug little farm the earth,
And see how his stock goes on.

Over the hill and over the dale,
And he went over the plain,
And backward and forward he switched his long tail
As a gentleman switches his cane.

And how then was the Devil dressed?
Oh! he was in his Sunday's best:
His jacket was red and his breeches were blue,
And there was a hole where the tail came through.

Samuel Taylor Coleridge
and Robert Southey

Some say the Deil's deid

Some say the Deil's deid,
The Deil's deid, the Deil's deid,
Some say the Deil's deid,
And buried in Kirkcaldy.

Some say he'll rise again,
Rise again, rise again,
Some say he'll rise again,
And dance the Hielan Laddie.

Unknown

The Flying Dutchman

We met the *Flying Dutchman*,
  By midnight he came,
His hull was all of hell fire,
  His sails were all aflame;
Fire on the main-top,
  Fire on the bow,
Fire on the gun-deck,
  Fire down below.

Four-and-twenty dead men,
  Those were the crew,
The Devil on the bowsprit,
  Fiddled as she flew.
We gave her the broadside,
  Right in the dip,
Just like a candle,
  Went out the ship.

Charles Godfrey Leland

No hiding place down there

A sinner man sat on the gates of hell,
A sinner man sat on the gates of hell,
A sinner man sat on the gates of hell,
The gates fell in and down he fell,
No hiding place down there.

I thought I heard my sister yell,
I thought I heard my sister yell,
I thought I heard my sister yell,
Way down deep in the middle of hell,
No hiding place down there.

I went to the rock to hide my face,
I went to the rock to hide my face,
I went to the rock to hide my face,
The rock called out, 'Go wash your face':
No hiding place down there.

Unknown

A linnet in hell

A linnet who had lost her way
Sang on a blackened bough in hell,
Till all the ghosts remembered well
The trees, the wind, the golden day.

At last they knew that they had died
When they heard music in that land,
And someone there stole forth a hand
To draw a brother to his side.

James Elroy Flecker

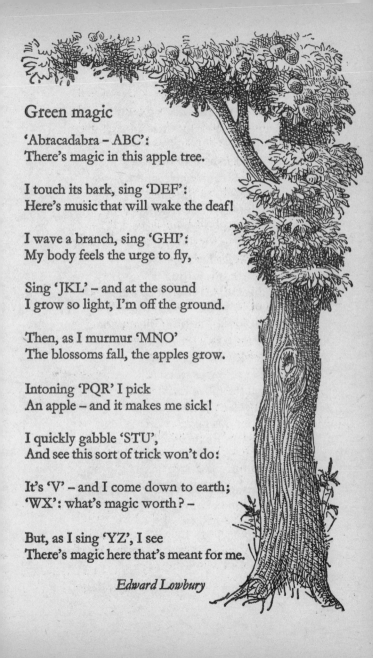

Green magic

'Abracadabra – ABC':
There's magic in this apple tree.

I touch its bark, sing 'DEF':
Here's music that will wake the deaf!

I wave a branch, sing 'GHI':
My body feels the urge to fly,

Sing 'JKL' – and at the sound
I grow so light, I'm off the ground.

Then, as I murmur 'MNO'
The blossoms fall, the apples grow.

Intoning 'PQR' I pick
An apple – and it makes me sick!

I quickly gabble 'STU',
And see this sort of trick won't do:

It's 'V' – and I come down to earth;
'WX': what's magic worth? –

But, as I sing 'YZ', I see
There's magic here that's meant for me.

Edward Lowbury

The Snitterjipe

In mellowy orchards, rich and ripe,
Is found the luminous Snitterjipe.
Bad boys who climb the bulging trees
Feel his sharp breath about their knees;
His trembling whiskers tickle so,
They squeak and squeal till they let go.
They hear his far-from-friendly bark;
They see his eyeballs in the dark
Shining and shifting in their sockets
As round and big as pears in pockets.
They feel his hot and wrinkly hide;
They see his nostrils flaming wide,
His tapering teeth, his jutting jaws,
His tongue, his tail, his twenty claws.
His hairy shadow in the moon
It makes them sweat, it makes them swoon;
And as they climb the orchard wall,
They let their pilfered pippins fall.
The Snitterjipe suspends pursuit
And falls upon the fallen fruit;
And while they flee the monster fierce,
Apples, not boys, his talons pierce.
With thumping hearts they hear him munch –
Six apples at a time he'll crunch.
At length he falls asleep, and they
On tiptoe take their homeward way.
But long before the blackbirds pipe
To welcome day, the Snitterjipe
Has fled afar, and on the green
Only his fearsome prints are seen.

James Reeves

'Be a monster'

I am a frightful monster,
My face is cabbage green
And even with my mouth shut
My teeth can still be seen.
My finger-nails are like rats' tails
And very far from clean.

I cannot speak a language
But make a wailing sound.
It could be any corner
You find me coming round.
Then, arms outspread and eyeballs red,
I skim across the ground.

The girls scream out and scatter
From this girl-eating bat.
I usually catch a small one
Because her legs are fat;
Or it may be she's tricked by me
Wearing her grandpa's hat.

Roy Fuller

The white monster

Last night I saw the monster near; the big
White monster that was like a lazy slug,
That hovered in the air, not far away,
As quiet as the black hawk seen by day.
I saw it turn its body round about,
And look my way; I saw its big, fat snout
Turn straight towards my face, till I was one
In coldness with that statue made of stone,
The one-armed sailor seen upon my right –
With no more power than he to offer fight;
The great white monster slug that, even then,
Killed women, children, and defenceless men.
But soon its venom was discharged, and it,
Knowing it had no more the power to spit
Death on the most defenceless English folk,
Let out a large, thick cloud of its own smoke;
And when the smoke had cleared away from there,
I saw no sign of any monster near;
And nothing but the stars to give alarm –
That never did the earth a moment's harm.
Oh, it was strange to see a thing like jelly,
An ugly, boneless thing all back and belly,
Among the peaceful stars – that should have been
A mile deep in the sea, and never seen:
A big, fat, lazy slug that, even then,
Killed women, children, and defenceless men.

W. H. Davies

The monster

When the sea-monster came to visit us,
Grey harbour-filling bulk with hungry head,
Although our shuddering hundreds ran to stare
In terror on his glaucous length, or pray
Where the sea boiled around him to the shore,
We were not properly prepared for such
An advent: no virgins could be found
Of the right age to satisfy the beast.

Although enthusiastic citizens
Threw fat babies, doddering grandparents,
Nubile non-virgins into the broth of sea
Around him, the monster snorted once
To show his great displeasure, and withdrew
The enormous serpentinings of his body
Over the horizon, leaving the town to mourn
Its inability to make a sacrifice,
And wonder what it is we want of monsters.

T. Harri Jones

The giant

Fee, fie, fo, fum!
I smell the blood of an English man.
Be he alive, or be he dead,
I'll grind his bones to make my bread.

Unknown

More about Blunderbore

It seems the giant Blunderbore
Is taller than a human door.
In fact, suppose him waiting to come in
All that you'd see would be a boot and shin.

But usually it's someone else
When we get up to answer bells.
And even were it actually giant B
He'd not push in much farther than his knee.

The following are the times or places
To guard against his hideous faces
(Or, more particularly, his appetite,
Which takes in children at a casual bite):

When climbing any garden tree
That's shot up rather suddenly;
Seeing a figure with a second head;
Or switching off the light to go to bed.

Roy Fuller

Giant Thunder

Giant Thunder, striding home,
Wonders if his supper's done.

'Hag wife, hag wife, bring me my bones!'
'They are not done,' the old hag moans.

'Not done? not done?' the giant roars
And heaves his old wife out of doors.

Cries he, 'I'll have them, cooked or not!'
But overturns the cooking-pot.

He flings the burning coals about;
See how the lightning flashes out!

Upon the gale the old hag rides,
The cloudy moon for terror hides.

All the world with thunder quakes;
Forest shudders, mountain shakes;
From the cloud the rainstorm breaks;
Village ponds are turned to lakes;
Every living creature wakes.

Hungry Giant, lie you still!
Stamp no more from hill to hill –
Tomorrow you shall have your fill.

James Reeves

The Ogre

'Tis moonlight on Trebarwith Sands,
  And moonlight on their seas,
Lone in a cove a cottage stands
  Enclustered in with trees.

Snuffing its thin faint smoke afar
  An Ogre prowls, and he
Smells supper; for where humans are,
  Rich dainties too may be.

Sweet as a larder to a mouse,
  So to him staring down,
Seemed the small-windowed moonlit house,
  With jasmine overgrown.

He snorted, as the billows snort
  In darkness of the night,
Betwixt his lean locks tawny-swart
  He glowered on the sight.

Into the garden sweet with peas
    He put his wooden shoe,
And bending back the apple trees
    Crept covetously through;

Then, stooping, with an impious eye
    Stared through the lattice small,
And spied two children which did lie
    Asleep, against the wall.

Into their dreams no shadow fell
    Of his disastrous thumb
Groping discreet, and gradual,
    Across the quiet room.

But scarce his nail had scraped the cot
    Wherein these children lay,
As if his malice were forgot,
    It suddenly did stay.

For faintly in the ingle-nook
    He heard a cradle-song,
That rose into his thoughts and woke
    Terror them among.

For she who in the kitchen sat
    Darning by the fire,
Guileless of what he would be at,
    Sang sweet as wind or wire:

'Lullay, thou little tiny child
    By-by, lullay, lullie;
Jesu in glory, meek and mild,
    This night remember thee!

'Fiend witch, and goblin, foul and wild,
    He deems them smoke to be;
Lullay, thou little tiny child,
    By-by, lullay, lullie!'

The Ogre lifted up his eyes
    Into the moon's pale ray,
And gazed upon her leopard-wise,
    Cruel and clear as day;

He snarled in gluttony and fear –
    The wind blows dismally –
'Jesu in storm my lambs be near,
    By-by, lullay, lullie!'

And like a ravenous beast which sees
    The hunter's icy eye,
So did this wretch in wrath confess
    Sweet Jesu's mastery.

With gaunt locks dangling, crouched he, then
    Drew backward from his prey,
Through tangled apple-boughs again
    He wrenched and rent his way.

Out on Trebarwith Sands he broke,
    The waves yelled back his cry,
Gannet and cormorant echo woke
    As he went striding by.

                        Walter de la Mare

Night wanderers

They hear the bell of midnight toll,
And shiver in their flesh and soul;
They lie on hard, cold wood or stone,
Iron, and ache in every bone;
They hate the night: they see no eyes
Of loved ones in the starlit skies.
They see the cold, dark water near;
They dare not take long looks for fear
They'll fall like those poor birds that see
A snake's eyes staring at their tree.
Some of them laugh, half-mad; and some
All through the chilly night are dumb;
Like poor, weak infants some converse,
And cough like giants, deep and hoarse.

W. H. Davies

Mab, the fairy queen

Come follow, follow me,
You, fairy elves that be:
Which circle on the green,
Come follow Mab, your queen.
Hand in hand let's dance around,
For this place is fairy ground,

When mortals are at rest,
And snoring in their nest;
Unheard and unespied,
Through keyholes we do glide;
Over tables, stools and shelves,
We trip it with our fairy elves.

And if the house be foul
With platter, dish or bowl,
Upstairs we nimbly creep,
And find the sluts asleep:
There we pinch their arms and thighs:
None escapes, nor none espies.

But if the house be swept,
And from uncleanness kept,
We praise the household maid,
And duly she is paid:
For we use before we go
To drop a tester in her shoe.

Upon a mushroom's head
Our table-cloth we spread;
A grain of rye or wheat,
Is the food which we eat;
Pearly drops of dew we drink
In acorn cups filled to the brink.

The grasshopper, gnat and fly
Serve for our minstrelsy;
Grace said, we dance awhile,
And so the time is beguile,
And if the moon doth hide her head,
The glow-worm lights us home to bed.

On tops of dewy grass
So nimbly do we pass,
The young and tender stalk
Ne'er bends when we do walk;
Yet in the morning may be seen
Where we the night before have been.

Unknown

Dryads

When meadows are grey with the morn
  In the dusk of the woods it is night:
The oak and the birch and the pine
  War with the glimmer of light.

Dryads brown as the leaf
  Move in the gloom of the glade;
When meadows are grey with the morn
  Dim night in the wood has delayed.

The cocks that crow to the land
  Are faint and hollow and shrill:
Dryads brown as the leaf
  Whisper, and hide, and are still.

Siegfried Sassoon

The little elf-man

I met a little elf-man once
Down where the lilies blow.
I asked him why he was so small,
And why he didn't grow.

He slightly frowned, and with his eye
He looked me through and through –
'I'm just as big for me,' said he,
'As you are big for you!'

J. K. Bangs

The satyr's catch

Buzz, quoth the blue fly,
  Hum, quoth the bee:
Buzz and hum, they cry,
  And so do we.
In his ear, in his nose,
  Thus, do you see?
He ate the dormouse,
  Else it was he.

Ben Jonson

The Werewolf

(*Written for the 1941 Hollywood film* The Wolf Man)

Even a man who is pure in heart,
And says his prayers by night,
May become a wolf when the wolfsbane blooms
And the autumn moon is bright.

Curt Siodmak

The Spunky

The Spunky he went like a sad little flame,
All, all alone.
All out on the zogs and a-down the lane,
All, all alone.
A tinker came by that was full of ale,
And into the mud he went head over tail,
All, all alone.

A crotchety farmer came riding by,
All, all alone.
He cursed him low and he cursed him high,
All, all alone.
The Spunky he up and he led him a-stray,
The pony were foundered until it were day,
All, all alone.

There came an old granny – she see the small ghost,
All, all alone.
'Yew poor liddle soul all a-cold, a-lost,
All, all alone.
I'll give 'ee a criss-cross to save 'ee bide;
Be off to the church and make merry inside,
All, all alone.'

The Spunky he laughed, 'Here I'll galley no more!'
All, all alone.
And off he did wiver and in at the door,
All, all alone.
The souls they did sing for to end his pain,
There's no little Spunky a-down the lane,
All, all alone.

Unknown

The phantom pumpkin

You may not believe it, for hardly could I:
I was cutting a pumpkin to put in a pie,
And on it was written in letters most plain
'You may hack me in slices, but I'll grow again.'

I seized it and sliced it and made no mistake
As, with dough rounded over, I put it to bake:
But soon in the garden as I chanced to walk,
Why, there was that pumpkin entire on his stalk!

Robert Graves

'Her strong enchantments failing . . .'

Her strong enchantments failing,
  Her towers of fear in wreck,
Her limbecks dried of poisons
  And the knife at her neck,

The Queen of air and darkness
  Begins to shrill and cry,
'O young man, O my slayer,
  Tomorrow you shall die.'

O Queen of air and darkness,
  I think 'tis truth you say,
And I shall die tomorrow;
  But you will die today.

A. E. Housman

The horror of Don't Care

Don't Care didn't care,
Don't Care was wild,
Don't Care stole plum and pear
Like any beggar's child.

Don't Care was made to care,
Don't Care was hung.
Don't Care was put in a pot
And boiled till he was done.

Unknown

Siesta

She went to bed
To doze,
And rose
To find that she was dead –
How, no one knows.

Stevie Smith

A dream of hanging

He rang me up
In a dream,
My brother did.
He had been hanged
That morning,
Innocent,
And I had slept
Through the striking
Of the clock
While it had taken place,
Eight,
Just about time enough
For it to happen.
He spoke to me
On the telephone
That afternoon
To reassure me,
My dear brother
Who had killed nobody,
And I asked him,
Long distance,
What it had felt like
To be hanged.
'Oh, don't worry, lovey', he said,
'When your time comes.
It tickled rather.'

Patricia Beer

Otis Snift –

a goblin funeral director

I'm a Goblin Mortician,
That's why I'm wearing black,
I drive 'em off to the graveyard
But I never bring 'em back.

People are quite tearful
When relatives end their day
But honestly, it cheers me up
To see 'em drive away.

And now I give the reason
I say it with misgiving:
To some people what they call death
I will call a living.

Spike Milligan

Her-zie

*(A troll and his wife speak of the human
child they stole)*

What's wrong with you-zie?
Nothing with me-zie.
Then what with who-zie?
Only with Her-zie.
So what with Her-zie?
A hearse for her-zie,
A hearse for her-zie
Came for her.

What colour was it then?
Golden, golden.
Was there anyone in it?
A pale king was in it.
That was not a hearse for Her-zie, husband,
It was her marriage carriage.
It was a hearse for me, then,
My heart went with them and died then.

Husband, ah me-zie,
Your heart has died for Her-zie,
Without it you cannot be easy.

Stevie Smith

Mr Ody met a body

Mr Ody met a body
Hanging from a tree;
And what was worse
He met a hearse
As black as black could be.
Mr Ody said 'By God, he
Ought to have a ride.'
Said the driver 'I'd oblige yer,
But we're full inside.'

Edith Nesbit

Ah, are you digging on my grave?

'Ah, are you digging on my grave,
    My loved one? – planting rue?'
—'No: yesterday he went to wed
One of the brightest wealth has bred.
"It cannot hurt her now", he said,
    "That I should not be true." '

'Then who is digging on my grave?
    My nearest dearest kin?'
—'Ah, no: they sit and think, "What use!
What good will planting flowers produce?
No tendance of her mound can loose
    Her spirit from Death's gin." '

'But some one digs upon my grave?
        My enemy? – prodding sly?'
—'Nay: when she heard you had passed the Gate
That shuts on all flesh soon or late,
She thought you no more worth her hate,
        And cares not where you lie.'

'Then, who is digging on my grave?
        Say – since I have not guessed!'
—"O it is I, my mistress dear,
Your little dog, who still lives near,
And much I hope my movements here
        Have not disturbed your rest?'

'Ah, yes! *You* dig upon my grave. . . .
        Why flashed it not on me
That one true heart was left behind!
What feeling do we ever find
To equal among human kind
        A dog's fidelity!'

'Mistress, I dug upon your grave
        To bury a bone, in case
I should be hungry near this spot
When passing on my daily trot.
I am sorry, but I quite forgot
        It was your resting-place.'

Thomas Hardy

Grave by a holm-oak

You lie there, Anna,
In your grave now,
Under a snow-sky,
You lie there now.

Where have the dead gone?
Where do they live now?
Not in the grave, they say,
Then where now?

Tell me, tell me,
Is it where I may go?
Ask not, cries the holm-oak,
Weep, says snow.

Stevie Smith

The unquiet grave

'The wind doth blow today, my love,
   And a few small drops of rain;
I never had but one true-love,
   In cold grave she was lain.

'I'll do as much for my true-love
    As any young man may;
I'll sit and mourn all at her grave
    For a twelvemonth and a day.'

The twelvemonth and a day being up,
    The dead began to speak:
'Oh who sits weeping on my grave,
    And will not let me sleep?'

''Tis I, my love, sits on your grave,
    And will not let you sleep;
For I crave one kiss of your clay-cold lips,
    And that is all I seek.'

'You crave one kiss of my clay-cold lips;
    But my breath smells earthly strong;
If you have one kiss of my clay-cold lips,
    Your time will not be long.'

' 'Tis down in yonder garden green,
    Love, where we used to walk,
The finest flower that ere was seen
    Is withered to a stalk.'

'The stalk is withered dry, my love,
    So will our hearts decay;
So make yourself content, my love,
    Till God calls you away.'

Unknown

To a human skeleton

(Encountered in the Museum of Natural History)

It's hard to think,
   Albeit true,
That without flesh
   I'd be like you.

And harder still
   To think, old pal,
That one of these
   Fine days I shall.

Richard Armour

The ghost and the skeleton

A skeleton once in Khartoum
Invited a ghost to his room.
   They spent the whole night
   In the eeriest fight
As to who should be frightened of whom.

Unknown

Two's company

The sad story of the man who didn't believe in ghosts

They said the house was haunted, but
He laughed at them and said, 'Tut, tut!
I've never heard such tittle-tattle
As ghosts that groan and chains that rattle;
And just to prove I'm in the right,
Please leave me here to spend the night.'

They winked absurdly, tried to smother
Their ignorant laughter, nudged each other,
And left him just as dusk was falling
With a hunchback moon and screech-owls calling.
Not that this troubled him one bit;
In fact, he was quite glad of it,
Knowing it's every sane man's mission
To contradict all superstition.

But what is that? Outside it seemed
As if chains rattled, someone screamed!
Come, come, it's merely nerves, he's certain
(But just the same, he draws the curtain).
The stroke of twelve – but there's no clock!
He shuts the door and turns the lock
(Of course, he knows that no one's there,
But no harm's done by taking care!)
Someone's outside – the silly joker,
(He may as well pick up the poker!)
That noise again! He checks the doors,
Shutters the windows, makes a pause

To seek the safest place to hide –
(The cupboard's strong – he creeps inside).
'Not that there's anything to fear,'
He tells himself, when at his ear
A voice breathes softly, 'How do you do!
I am the ghost. Pray, who are you?'

Raymond Wilson

Ghosts

1
The scrubbed, magnificently decked coffin
Skates, like a new ship, into the fiery deep.
On dry land,
The congregation rustles to its knees.

2
From my corner pew
I command an unobstructed view
Of your departure.
If you had been lying on your side
I might have caught your unsuspecting eye.

3
Out on the patio, at dusk,
The floral tributes. I could almost swear
That it was you I saw
Sniffing the wreath-scented air
And counting the bowed heads of your bereaved.

Ian Hamilton

Sweet William's ghost

There came a ghost to Margret's door,
   With many a grievous groan,
And then he knocked upon the door,
   But answer made she none.

'Is that my father Philip?
   Or is it my brother John?
Or is it my true love Willie,
   From Scotland now come home?'

'It's not your father Philip,
   It's not your brother John,
But it's your true love Willie,
   From Scotland now come home.

'O sweet Margret! O dear Margret!
   I pray you speak to me;
Give me faith and love, Margret,
   As I gave it to thee.'

'That faith and love you'll never get,
   That prize you'll never win,
Until you come inside my house
   And kiss my cheek and chin.'

Old English ballad

The ghost's lament

Woe's me, woe's me,
The acorn's not yet
Fallen from the tree,
That's to grow the oak
That's to make the cradle,
That's to rock the bairn,
That's to grow a man
That's to lay me.

Unknown

Eerie men of Erith

There are men in the village of Erith
Whom nobody seeth or heareth,
   And there looms on the marge
   Of the river a barge
That nobody roweth or steereth.

Unknown

Albert and the ghost of Lady Jane Grey

On young Albert Ramsbottom's birthday
   His parents asked what he'd like most;
He said to see t' Tower of London
   And gaze upon Anne Boleyn's ghost.

They thowt this request were unusual,
  And at first to refuse were inclined,
Till Pa said a trip to t' metrollopse
  Might broaden the little lad's mind.

They took charrybank up to London
  And got there at quarter to fower,
Then seeing as pubs wasn't open
  They went straight away to the Tower.

They didn't think much to the building,
  'T weren't what they'd been led to suppose,
And the 'Bad Word' Tower didn't impress them,
  They said Blackpool had got one of those.

At last Albert found a Beefeater,
  And filled the old chap with alarm
By asking for ghost of Anne Boleyn,
  As carried her head 'neath her arm.

Said Beefeater, 'You ought to come Fridays
   If it's ghost of Anne Boleyn you seek,
Her Union now limits her output,
   And she only gets one walk a week.'

'But,' he said, 'if it's ghosts that you're after,
   There's Lady Jane Grey's to be seen,
She runs around chased by the 'Eadsman
   At midnight on th' old Tower Green.'

They waited on t' green till near midnight,
   Then thinking they'd time for a sup,
They took out what food they'd brought with them
   And waited for t' ghost to turn up.

G. Marriott Edgar

Once I was a monarch's daughter

Once I was a monarch's daughter,
And sat on a lady's knee:
But now I am a nightly rover
Banished to the ivy tree.

Crying *hoo, hoo, hoo, hoo, hoo,*
Hoo, hoo, hoo, my feet are cold.

Pity me, for here you see me
Persecuted, poor, and old.

Unknown

The ghosts' high noon

When the night wind howls in the chimney cowls,
          and the bat in the moonlight flies,
And inky clouds, like funeral shrouds, sail over the
             midnight skies –
When the footpads quail at the night-bird's wail, and
          black dogs bay the moon,
Then is the spectres' holiday – then is the ghosts'
             high noon!

As the sob of the breeze sweeps over the trees, and
          the mists lie low on the fen,
From grey tombstones are gathered the bones that
          once were women and men,
And away they go, with a mop and a mow, to the
          revel that ends too soon,
For cockcrow limits our holiday – the dead of the
            night's high noon!

And then each ghost with his ladye-toast to their
          churchyard beds take flight,
With a kiss, perhaps, on her lantern chaps, and a
            grisly grim 'good night';
Till the welcome knell of the midnight bell rings
          forth its jolliest tune,
And ushers our next high holiday – the dead of the
            night's high noon!

W. S. Gilbert

Song of two ghosts

My friend
This is a wide world
We're travelling over
Walking on the moonlight.

Indian song from Omaha,
North America

The great auk's ghost

The great auk's ghost rose on one leg,
   Sighed thrice and three times winkt,
And turned and poached a phantom egg,
   And muttered, 'I'm extinct.'

Ralph Hodgson

There she weaves by night and day

(from The Lady of Shalott*)*

There she weaves by night and day
A magic web with colours gay.
She has heard a whisper say,
A curse is on her if she stay
       To look down to Camelot.
She knows not what the curse may be,
And so she weaveth steadily,
And little other care hath she,
       The Lady of Shalott.

And moving through a mirror clear
That hangs before her all the year,
Shadows of the world appear.
There she sees the highway near
       Winding down to Camelot:
There the river eddy whirls,
And there the surly village-churls,
And the red cloaks of market girls,
       Pass onward from Shalott.

Sometimes a troop of damsels glad,
An abbot on an ambling pad,
Sometimes a curly shepherd-lad,
Or long-haired page in crimson clad,
       Goes by to towered Camelot;
And sometimes through the mirror blue
The knights come riding two and two:
She hath no loyal knight and true,
       The Lady of Shalott.

But in her web she still delights
To weave the mirror's magic sights,
For often through the silent nights
A funeral, with plumes and lights,
    And music, went to Camelot;
Or when the moon was overhead,
Came two young lovers lately wed;
'I am half sick of shadows,' said
        The Lady of Shalott.

Alfred, Lord Tennyson

Sir Roger

(*You can read this poem to the tune and rhythm of the familiar folk song* Here we go round the mulberry bush.)

Sir Roger is dead and low in his grave,
Low in his grave, low in his grave.
Sir Roger is dead and low in his grave,
Hey! High! Low in his grave.

They planted an apple-tree over his head,
Over his head, over his head.
They planted an apple-tree over his head,
Hey! High! Over his head.

The apples got ripe and they all fell off,
All fell off, all fell off.
The apples got ripe and they all fell off,
Hey! High! All fell off.

There came an old woman a-picking them up,
A-picking them up, a-picking them up.
There came an old woman a-picking them up,
Hey! High! A-picking them up.

Sir Roger got up and he gave her a nudge,
Gave her a nudge, gave her a nudge.
Sir Roger got up and he gave her a nudge,
Hey! High! Gave her a nudge.

It made the old woman go hippety-hop,
Hippety-hop, hippety-hop.
It made the old woman go hippety-hop,
Hey! High! Hippety-hop.

Unknown

Windy nights

Whenever the moon and stars are set,
    Whenever the wind is high,
All night long in the dark and wet,
    A man goes riding by.
Late in the night when the fires are out,
Why does he gallop and gallop about?

Whenever the trees are crying aloud,
    And ships are tossed at sea,
By, on the highway, low and loud,
    By at the gallop goes he:
By at the gallop he goes, and then
By he comes back at the gallop again.

Robert Louis Stevenson

The Crooked Pear Tree Hill

Under the hill there burns a fire
That reddens first December snow;
Puffing his pipe, the watchman sees
The stream of life that comes and goes,
And in the shrouded darkness fades
To leave him nodding through the night.
He crouches there, his shoulders hung
With heavy sacks to stay the cold;
His hut, a little house of white,
Lies just beyond the lamp's raw glare.
And sitting by him in the dark
Beneath a sky of hidden stars,
I heard him tell this fearful tale
As only he, the watchman, could,
With ghostly voice and nervous hands:

'I shall be sixty-nine on New Year's Day,
A roadman for nigh fifty years;
'Twas when I was a youngish chap
That this did happen which I tell;
It was a night as strange as this
And I was on this very road,
Not far from Littledean, and near
The Greyhound Inn and Chestnut Woods,
And black before me loomed this hill
Where once fat orchards flowered
And cottage smoke twirled up through fern,
The fatal Crooked Pear Tree Hill.
The snow was slipping down, the chimes
Went dumb in far-off Newnham Tower,
And everything went dead save when
Some waking owl screeched out his name

Or drunken men went lurching by
Half singing to the heedless stars.
And there I sat untroubled till
The night began to turn at twelve
And then, quite faint, I thought I heard
The jingling of some merry bells,
The sound of trotting horses' hoofs,
And soon there drove around the bend
An ancient coach with four fine bays,
The like I'd never seen before.
I rubbed my eyes, but plain enough
I saw it coming nearer me;
There up in front was perched a man
Holding the traces in thin hands,
Once round the corner up he pulled
And halted by the dark roadside.
I saw three other men get out
Who wore three-cornered hats, and coats
Up to their chins, and leathern gloves,
With jack-boots well up to the knees.
I minded how my father said
The coaches ran from Gloucester town
When he was but a tiny lad
And George the Fourth was ruling king,
To Chepstow, every twice the week,
And how at Elton they would leave
The main road for to pick up those
Who journeyed out from Littledean,
And after waiting at the "George"
Would take the onward route again.

'Then by their lantern's flickering gleam
They started quarrelling as they stood,
But what 'twas all about and why,

I could not very well make out
Till one whipped out his naked sword
And there beneath the freezing sky
Two of them fought with panting breath:
I saw them with their flashing steels
Lunge at each other, parry strokes
That sent the fire along their blades,
Until one slithered on the road
When quick as anything, his foe
Had pushed his weapon through and through
His adversary's quivering breast.
And slow he sank upon his knees,
And slow he gasped away his breath,
And slow his blood stained all the snow.
And then I saw a gruesome thing
Which chilled the marrow in my bones

And sent the sweat along my brows;
I saw them hack with chopping swords
His curl-crowned head off at the neck
As if to hide their wretched guilt.
One cried "A traitor's life is done."
Another "Now we have the gold."
They flung the body, head and all,
Into the ditch beneath the hedge
And having done, stepped in the coach
Which swung off through the deep'ning snow
Till silent were the tossing bells
And hushed the cracking of the whip.

'At last I stirred my trembling self
Which up to then had powerless been
To raise a hand to stop the fray,
(But here the queerness of this tale
Which you or any may not heed
Although I know what I did see;)
When I walked over to the place
And looked upon the murdered ground,
It was not trampled on at all,
There was no blood upon the snow
Or marks of horses or of men.

'But still at Christmas time he comes
In phantom form, that nameless man,
To haunt this very road alone
At midnight's sad and sombre hour;
He, headless, walks with head in hand
His curls fast flying in the wind
Over the Crooked Pear Tree Hill.'

Leonard Clark

Shadwell Stair

I am the ghost of Shadwell Stair.
  Along the wharves by the water-house,
  And through the dripping slaughter-house,
I am the shadow that walks there.

Yet I have flesh both firm and cool,
  And eyes tumultuous as the gems
  Of moons and lamps in the lapping Thames
When dusk sails wavering down the pool.

Shuddering the purple street-arc burns
  Where I watch always; from the banks
  Dolorously the shipping clanks,
And after me a strange tide turns.

I walk till the stars of London wane
  And dawn creeps up the Shadwell Stair.
  But when the crowing sirens blare
I with another ghost am lain.

Wilfred Owen

Colonel Fazackerley

Colonel Fazackerley Butterworth-Toast
Bought an old castle complete with a ghost,
But someone or other forgot to declare
To Colonel Fazack that the spectre was there.

On the very first evening, while waiting to dine,
The Colonel was taking a fine sherry wine,
When the ghost, with a furious flash and a flare,
Shot out of the chimney and shivered, 'Beware!'

Colonel Fazackerley put down his glass
And said, 'My dear fellow, that's really first class!
I just can't conceive how you do it at all.
I imagine you're going to a Fancy Dress Ball?'

At this, the dread ghost gave a withering cry.
Said the Colonel (his monocle firm in his eye),
'Now just how you do it I wish I could think.
Do sit down and tell me, and please have a drink.'

The ghost in his phosphorous cloak gave a roar
And floated about between ceiling and floor.
He walked through a wall and returned through a
pane
And backed up the chimney and came down again.

Said the Colonel, 'With laughter I'm feeling quite
weak!'
(As trickles of merriment ran down his cheek).
'My house-warming party I hope you won't spurn.
You *must* say you'll come and you'll give us a turn!'

At this, the poor spectre – quite out of his wits –
Proceeded to shake himself almost to bits.
He rattled his chains and he clattered his bones
And he filled the whole castle with mumbles and
moans.

But Colonel Fazackerley, just as before,
Was simply delighted and called out, 'Encore!'
At which the ghost vanished, his efforts in vain,
And never was seen at the castle again.

'Oh dear, what a pity!' said Colonel Fazack.
'I don't know his name, so I can't call him back.'
And then with a smile that was hard to define,
Colonel Fazackerley went in to dine.

Charles Causley

The ghost in the garden

For clanking and lank
The Armoured Knight
Rides down the dank
Shadows in flight;
Grass stiff with frost
Shows grey as steel
As the Conquering Ghost
Clanks down the hill.
    Now the first cock crows,
    Impudent, frightened, through the dark;
    Then a cold wind blows,
    And that whining dog, Dawn, begins to bark.
Then the Knight in Armour
Passes away,
As the growing clamour
Proclaims, 'It is Day'.
The trees grow taller,
The gate is shut,
The Knight grows smaller,
             Goes smaller,
                And out.

Osbert Sitwell

Ghosts

I to a crumpled cabin came
Upon a hillside high,
And with me was a withered dame
As weariful as I.
'It used to be our home,' said she;
'How I remember well!
Oh that our happy hearth should be
Today an empty shell!'

The door was flailing in the storm
That deafed us with its din;
The roof that kept us once so warm
Now let the snow-drift in.
The floor sagged to the sod below,
The walls caved crazily;
We only heard the wind of woe
Where once was glow and glee.

So there we stood disconsolate
Beneath the Midnight Dome,
An ancient miner and his mate,
Before our wedded home,
Where we had known such love and cheer . . .
I sighed, then soft she said:
'Do not regret – remember, dear,
                    We, too, are dead.'

                                        Robert Service

The phantom-lover

A ghost, that loved a lady fair,
Ever in the starry air
   Of midnight at her pillow stood;
And, with a sweetness skies above
The luring words of human love,
   Her soul the phantom wooed.
Sweet and sweet is their poisoned note,
The little snakes of silver throat,
In mossy skulls that nest and lie,
Ever singing 'die, oh! die'.

Young soul put off your flesh, and come
With me into the quiet tomb,
   Our bed is lovely, dark, and sweet;
The earth will swing us, as she goes,
Beneath our coverlid of snows,
   And the warm leaden sheet.
Dear and dear is their poisoned note,
The little snakes of silver throat,
In mossy skulls that nest and lie,
Ever singing 'die, oh! die'.

Thomas Lovell Beddoes

Shadow-bride

There was a man who dwelt alone,
   as day and night went past
he sat as still as carven stone,
   and yet no shadow cast.
The white owls perched upon his head
   beneath the winter moon;
they wiped their beaks and thought him dead
   under the stars of June.

There came a lady clad in grey
   in the twilight shining:
one moment she would stand and stay,
   her hair with flowers entwining.
He woke, as had he sprung of stone,
   and broke the spell that bound him;
he clasped her fast, both flesh and bone,
   and wrapped her shadow round him.

There never more she walks her ways
   by sun or moon or star;
she dwells below where neither days
   nor any nights there are.
But once a year when caverns yawn
   and hidden things awake,
they dance together then till dawn
   and a single shadow make.

J. R. R. Tolkien

The handkerchief ghost

There is a ghost
That eats handkerchiefs;
It keeps you company
On all your travels, and
Eats your handkerchiefs
Out of your trunk, your
Bed, your washstand,
Like a bird eating
Out of your hand – not
All of them and not
All at one go. With
Eighteen handkerchiefs
You set out, a proud mariner,
On the Seas of the Unknown;
With eight or perhaps
Seven you come back, the
Despair of the housewife.

Christian Morgenstern

The ghost

'Who knocks?' 'I, who was beautiful,
   Beyond all dreams to restore,
I, from the roots of the dark thorn am hither.
   And knock on the door.'

'Who speaks?' 'I – once was my speech
   Sweet as the bird's on the air,
When echo lurks by the waters to heed;
   'Tis I speak thee fair.'

'Dark is the hour!' 'Ay, and cold.'
   'Lone is my house.' 'Ah, but mine?'
'Sight, touch, lips, eyes yearned in vain.'
   'Long dead these to thine. . . .'

Silence. Still faint on the porch
   Brake the flames of the stars.
In gloom groped a hope-wearied hand
   Over keys, bolts, and bars.

A face peered. All the grey night
   In chaos of vacancy shone;
Nought but vast sorrow was there –
   The sweet cheat gone.

                           Walter de la Mare

The glimpse

She sped through the door
And, following in haste,
And stirred to the core,
I entered hot-faced;
But I could not find her,
No sign was behind her.
'Where is she?' I said:
– 'Who?' they asked that sat there;
'Not a soul's come in sight.'
– 'A maid with red hair.'
– 'Ah.' They paled. 'She is dead.
People see her at night,
But you are the first
On whom she has burst
In the keen common light.'

It was ages ago,
When I was quite strong:
I have waited since – O,
I have waited so long!
– Yea, I set me to own
The house, where now alone
I dwell in void rooms
Booming hollow as tombs!
But I never come near her,
Though nightly, I hear her.
And my cheek has grown thin
And my hair has grown gray
With this waiting therein;
But she still keeps away!

Thomas Hardy

Haunted

Through the imponderable twilight tumbles
  A fuzzy mass, uncertain at the edges.
This, so they tell me, is the ghost that grumbles,
  The spectre that goes backwards through the
                                    hedges.

The goblin garrulous but rarely witty,
  The harmless phantom and the wraith endearing,
That hops around and sings a tuneless ditty
  And interrupts himself with bursts of cheering;

A spirit fairly lovable, and decent.
  Some say he is the shade of Charles the Martyr;
Others incline to a demise more recent,
  Claiming he is a Mr Eustace Carter,

A man who flourished here in eighteen-fifty
  And fell into a pond while trapping rabbits.
At all events, although a trifle shifty,
  The spectre has few irritating habits,

Never comes after dark, but in the twilight,
  And rarely frightens people, or not badly,
But sits in summer evenings on the skylight,
  Scratching himself, and singing, rather sadly.

R. P. Lister

Prince Kano

In a dark wood Prince Kano lost his way
And searched in vain through the long summer's day.
At last, when night was near, he came in sight
Of a small clearing filled with yellow light,
And there, bending beside his brazier, stood
A charcoal burner wearing a black hood.
The Prince cried out for joy: 'Good friend, I'll give
What you will ask: guide me to where I live.'
The man pulled back his hood: he had no face –
Where it should be there was an empty space.

Half dead with fear the Prince staggered away,
Rushed blindly through the wood till break of day;
And then he saw a larger clearing, filled
With houses, people, but his soul was chilled;
He looked around for comfort, and his search
Led him inside a small, half-empty church
Where monks prayed. 'Father,' to one he said,
'I've seen a dreadful thing; I am afraid.'
'What did you see, my son?' 'I saw a man
Whose face was like . . .' and, as the Prince began,
The monk drew back his hood and seemed to hiss,
Pointing to where his face should be, 'Like this?'

Edward Lowbury

Sally Simpkin's and John Jones's ghastly ghostly catastrophe

'Oh! what is that comes gliding in,
   And quite in middling haste?
It is the picture of my Jones,
   And painted to the waist.

'It is not painted to the life,
   For where's the trousers blue?
Oh, Jones, my dear! – Oh, dear! my Jones,
   What is become of you?'

'Oh, Sally dear, it is too true,
   The half that you remark
Is come to say my other half
   Is bit off by a shark!

'Oh! Sally, sharks do things by halves,
   Yet most completely do!
A bite in one place seems enough,
   But I've been bit in two.

'You know I once was all your own,
  But now a shark must share!
But let that pass – for now to you
  I'm neither here nor there.

'Alas! Death has a strange divorce
  Effected in the sea,
It has divided me from you,
  And even me from me.

'Don't fear my ghost will walk o' nights
  To haunt, as people say;
My ghost *can't* walk, for, oh! my legs
  Are many leagues away!

'Lord! think when I am swimming round
  And looking where the boat is,
A shark just snaps away a *half*
  Without "a *quarter's* notice".

'One half is here, the other half
  Is near Columbia placed;
Oh! Sally, I have got the whole
  Atlantic for my waist.

'But now, adieu – a long adieu!
  I've solved death's awful riddle,
And would say more, but I am doomed
  To break off in the middle!'

Thomas Hood

The old wife and the ghost

There was an old wife and she lived all alone
  In a cottage not far from Hitchin:
And one bright night, by the full moon light,
  Comes a ghost right into her kitchen.

About that kitchen neat and clean
  The ghost goes pottering round.
But the poor old wife is deaf as a boot
  And so hears never a sound.

The ghost blows up the kitchen fire,
  As bold as bold can be;
He helps himself from the larder shelf,
  But never a sound hears she.

He blows on his hands to make them warm,
  And whistles aloud 'Whee-hee!'
But still as a sack the old soul lies
  And never a sound hears she.

From corner to corner he runs about,
  And into the cupboard he peeps;
He rattles the door and bumps on the floor,
  But still the old wife sleeps.

Jangle and bang go the pots and pans,
  As he throws them all around;
And the plates and mugs and dishes and jugs,
  He flings them all to the ground.

Madly the ghost tears up and down
    And screams like a storm at sea;
And at last the old wife stirs in her bed –
    And it's 'Drat those mice,' says she.

Then the first cock crows and morning shows
    And the troublesome ghost's away.
But oh! what a pickle the poor wife sees
    When she gets up next day.

'Them's tidy big mice,' the old wife thinks,
    And off she goes to Hitchin,
And a tidy big cat she fetches back
    To keep the mice from her kitchen.

James Reeves

City

When the great bell
BOOMS over the Portland stone urn, and
From the carved cedar wood
Rises the odour of incense,
I SIT DOWN
In St Botolph Bishopsgate Churchyard
And wait for the spirit of my grandfather
Toddling along from the Barbican.

John Betjeman

The ghosts' walk

They came with lorries, they came with vans, they
came in the early May;
Room by room and stair by stair they carried the
house away;
There was never a brick and never a stone to show
where the old home stood,
And a couple of family ghosts were left who took to
a nearby wood.

The Northern Spring was a genial Spring, and the
summer nights were fair,
And the two ghosts walked in the gibbous moon and
danced in the open air.
Autumn came and they weren't so pleased, for the
wind waxed cold and keen.
And one of the two had a ghostly liver and one had a
phantom spleen.

One ghost said to the other ghost, 'Alas for the brave
                                    old days,
When the walls were strong in the house and the
                          fires had a cheerful blaze.'
And the second ghost answered tartly, 'That's a
                          fatheaded way to talk,
'When there isn't as much as a cupboard left where
                          an indoor ghost could walk.'

The rain dripped down from the naked boughs, the
                          wind swept in through the holes,
Their spinal columns were stiff and damp, and the
                          first said, 'Blast their souls;
A Tudor house in its early state might well have
                          been left intact.'
And the other sat on his hands and said, 'It wasn't,
                          and that's a fact.

'We might have got in the last sad van and gone
                          where the old house went;
We knew they were sticking it up afresh in Surrey or
                          Hants or Kent,
I'm not sure which; but stair by stair and room by
                          room it stands
Where I'd be now if it wasn't for you.' And again
                          he sat on his hands.

But mildly the first ghost answered, 'For centuries
                          close on nine,
Here we have been with our sons and sires, an
                          honoured and ancient line;
Think of the sentiment, Sniffey.' The second in
                          charnel tones
Said, 'Sentiment's all very well in its place, but
                          sentiment won't warm bones.'

And the wind swept in through the naked boles, and
                        the rain dripped down from the bough,
And the two ghosts huddled together – it was far
                              too cold for a row –
Till the strong ghost said, 'Here, up you!'; and, or
                          ever that storm was spent,
They were off on a trek from the cheerless North to
                        Surrey—or Hants—or Kent.

There's a fearsome story of two pale ghosts that the
                            horrified rustic meets
Stalking along by the Great North Road through the
                          villages' quiet streets;
Night by night one can mark their trail; we learn
                          from the last report
They've crossed the Thames by Wallingford Bridge,
                      but were going a trifle short.

John Kendall

Emperors of the island

There is the story of a deserted island
where five men walked down to the bay.

The story of the island is
that three men would two men slay.

Three men dug two graves in the sand,
three men stood on the sea wet rock,
three shadows moved away.

There is the story of a deserted island
where three men walked down to the bay.

The story of this island is
that two men would one man slay.

Two men dug one grave in the sand,
two men stood on the sea wet rock,
two shadows moved away.

There is the story of a deserted island
where two men walked down to the bay.

The story of this island is
that one man would one man slay.

One man dug one grave in the sand,
one man stood on the sea wet rock,
one shadow moved away.

There is the story of a deserted island
where four ghosts walked down to the bay.

The story of this island is
that four ghosts would one man slay.

Four ghosts dug one grave in the sand,
four ghosts stood on the sea wet rock;
five ghosts moved away.

Dannie Abse

The man who wasn't there

Yesterday upon the stair
I met the man who wasn't there;
He wasn't there again today,
I wish, I wish, he'd go away.

I've seen his shapeless shadow-coat
Beneath the stairway, hanging about;
And outside, muffled in a cloak
The same colour as the dark;

I've seen him in a black, black suit
Shaking, under the broken light;
I've seen him swim across the floor
And disappear beneath the door;

And once, I almost heard his breath
Behind me, running up the path:
Inside, he leant against the wall,
And turned . . . and was no one at all.

Yesterday upon the stair,
I met the man who wasn't there;
He wasn't there again today,
I wish, I wish, he'd go away.

Brian Lee

On a dentist

Stranger, approach this spot with gravity:
John Brown is filling his last cavity.

Unknown

On Leslie Moore

Here lies what's left
Of Leslie Moore –
   No Les
   No more.

Unknown

On Dr Chard

Here lies the corpse of Doctor Chard,
Who filled half of this churchyard.

Unknown

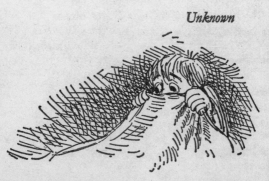

Index of titles

Index of first lines

Acknowledgements

The authors and publishers would like to thank the following people for giving permission to include in this anthology material which is their copyright. The publishers have made every effort to trace copyright holders. If we have inadvertently omitted to acknowledge anyone we should be grateful if this could be brought to our attention for correction at the first opportunity.

George Allen and Unwin Ltd for 'Shadow-bride' from *The Adventures of Tom Bombadil* by J. R. R. Tolkien.
Richard Armour for 'To a human skeleton' from *An Armoury of Light Verse*.
Ernest Benn Ltd for 'Ghosts' from the collection 'Lyrics of a Low Brow' in *More Collected Verse of Robert Service*.
Jonathan Cape Ltd and the estate of Robert Frost for 'House Fear' from *The Poetry of Robert Frost*, edited by Edward Connery Latham.
Jonathan Cape Ltd and the executors of the W. H. Davies estate for 'The White Monster' and 'Night Wanderers' from *The Complete Poems of W. H. Davies*.
Chatto and Windus Ltd and the Owen estate for 'Shadwell Stair' from *The Collected Poems of Wilfred Owen*.
Leonard Clark for 'The Crooked Pear Tree Hill' by Leonard Clark.
Coward, McCann and Geoghegan, Inc., for 'Daniel Webster's Horses' from *The Creaking Stair* by Elizabeth Coatsworth. Copyright 1923 by Elizabeth Coatsworth. Copyright 1929, 1949 by Coward-McCann, Inc.
Francis, Day and Hunter Ltd, 138–140 Charing Cross Road, London WC2H OLD for *Albert and the 'Eadsman* by G. Marriott Edgar.
J. M. Dent and Sons Ltd for 'The Haunted Child' from *Non-Stop Nonsense* by Margaret Mahy.
Andre Deutsch Ltd for 'Nasty Night', 'The Dark', 'Be a Monster', and 'More About Blunderbore' from *Poor Roy* by Roy Fuller.
Dobson Books Ltd for 'Bump' from *The Little Pot-boiler* by Spike Milligan, and for 'Hallowe'en' from *Good Company* by Leonard Clark.
Duckworth and Co Ltd for 'Kitchen Song' from *Façade and Other Poems* by Edith Sitwell; and for 'The Ghost in the Garden' from *Collected Satires and Poems* by Osbert Sitwell.
Faber and Faber Ltd, for extract from *The Family Reunion* by T. S. Eliot; and for 'The Riddle' and 'Bad Dream' from *The Collected Poems of Louis MacNeice*.
The Gomer Press (J. D. Lewis and Sons Ltd) for 'The Monster' by T. Harri Jones.
Robert Graves for 'Two Witches' from *Collected Poems* by Robert Graves, and 'The Phantom Pumpkin' by Robert Graves.
George G. Harrap and Co Ltd for 'The Ghosts' Walk' from *Selected Verses* by John Kendall.

William Heinemann Ltd for 'Moths and Moonshine' from *Ragged Robin* by James Reeves; for 'Old Moll' from *The Wandering Moon* by James Reeves; and for 'The Snitterjipe' from *Prefabulous Animiles* by James Reeves.

David Higham Associates and William Collins Sons & Co Ltd for 'The Witch's Work-Song' from *The Sword in the Stone* by T. H. White.

David Higham Associates Ltd and Macmillan and Co Ltd for 'Colonel Fazackerley' from *Figgie Hobbin* by Charles Causley.

Mrs Hodgson and Macmillan, London and Basingstoke, for 'The Great Auk's Ghost' from *Collected Poems* by Ralph Hodgson.

The Hogarth Press Ltd for 'Night Omens' from *Kilroy was Here* by John Cotton.

Hope Leresche and Sayle for *Gruesome* by Roger McGough; copyright © 1979 by Roger McGough, from *You Tell Me* (Kestrel Books).

Houghton Mifflin Company, New York, for 'Night Clouds' from *The Complete Works of Amy Lowell*, copyright 1955 by Houghton Mifflin Company, reprinted by permission of the publisher.

Hutchinson Publishing Group Ltd for 'Otis Snift – a goblin funeral director' from *Goblins* by Spike Milligan.

James Kirkup for 'Who's That?' by James Kirkup, from *Round About Nine* edited by Geoffrey Palmer and Noel Lloyd (Warne).

R. P. Lister for 'Haunted' from *The Idle Demon* by R. P. Lister (Deutsch).

Literary Trustees of Walter de la Mare and the Society of Authors as their representative for 'Eeka Neeka', 'I saw Three Witches', 'The Ghost', 'The Listeners', 'The Little Creature', 'The Ogre', and 'The Ride-by-Nights' from *The Complete Poems of Walter de la Mare*.

Edward Lowbury for 'Green Magic' and 'Prince Kano' from *Green Magic* (Chatto and Windus).

James MacGibbon, executor of the estate of Stevie Smith, for 'Grave by a Holm Oak', 'Her-zie' and 'Siesta' from *The Collected Poems of Stevie Smith* (Allen Lane).

Macmillan, London and Basingstoke, for 'The Little Elf-Man' by J. K. Bangs from *Rhyme and Rhythm Blue Book* by J. Gibson and R. Wilson; and for 'Two's Company' by Raymond Wilson from *Rhyme and Rhythm Yellow Book* by J. Gibson and R. Wilson.

John Murray Publishers Ltd for 'City' from *Collected Poems* by John Betjeman.

The National Trust and Macmillan London Ltd for 'The Eggshell' from *The Definitive Edition of Rudyard Kipling's Verse*.

James Nimmo for 'Space Traveller' by James Nimmo.

Oxford University Press for 'The Old Wife and the Ghost' and 'Giant Thunder' from *The Blackbird in the Lilac* by James Reeves.

Penguin Books Ltd for 'All on my own', 'The Queer Moment', 'Quite in the Dark', and 'The Man who wasn't there' from *Late Home* by Brian Lee.

Acknowledgements

Laurence Pollinger Ltd, and the estate of the late Mrs Frieda Lawrence Ravagli for 'The Witch' from *The Complete Poems of D. H. Lawrence*.
Sylvia Read for 'Owl' by Sylvia Read.
G. T. Sassoon for 'Dryads' by Siegfried Sassoon.
Ian Serraillier for 'The Witch's Cat' from *Happily Ever After*, and for 'Riddle', 'Spell' and 'The Two Ravens' from *I'll tell you a Tale*.
Anthony Sheil Associates Ltd for 'Emperors of the Island' from *Tenants of the House* (Hutchinson).
The Society of Authors as the literary representative of the estate of A. E. Housman, and Jonathan Cape Ltd, for 'Her Strong Enchantments Failing' by A. E. Housman.
John Wilson for 'A Witch's Chant' by John Wilson.
Mrs Iris Wise and Macmillan, London and Basingstoke, for 'In the Night' and 'The Turn of the Road' from *Collected Poems* by James Stephens.

201783